Where Words

Near and Far

by Tami Johnson

Capstone press®

Mankato, Minnesota

A+ Books are published by Capstone Press,
151 Good Counsel Drive, P.O. Box 669, Mankato, Minnesota 56002.
www.capstonepress.com

1 2 3 4 5 6 12 11 10 09 08 07

Library of Congress Cataloging-in-Publication Data
Johnson, Tami.
    Near and far / by Tami Johnson.
    p. cm. — (A+ books. Where words)
    Summary: "Simple text and color photographs introduce basic concepts of near
and far"—Provided by publisher.
    Includes bibliographical references and index.
    ISBN-13: 978-0-7368-6736-8 (hardcover)
    ISBN-10: 0-7368-6736-8 (hardcover)
    ISBN-13: 978-0-7368-7854-8 (softcover pbk.)
    ISBN-10: 0-7368-7854-8 (softcover pbk.)
    1. Space perception—Juvenile literature. I. Title. II. Series.
BF469.O7J64 2007
153.7'52—dc22   2006022807

Credits

Megan Schoeneberger, editor; Juliette Peters, designer; Charlene Deyle, photo researcher;
    Scott Thoms, photo editor

Photo Credits

2004 George Hall/Check Six, 17; Capstone Press/Karon Dubke, 14, 15, 29 (bottom); Corbis/Bettmann,
6; Corbis/Denis Scott, 26; Corbis/Frans Lanting, 8; Corbis/Jan Butchofsky-Houser, 13; Corbis/Joe
McDonald, 20; Corbis/NewSport/Andreas Neumeier, 7; Corbis/Owen Franken, 4–5; Corbis/Philip James
Corwin, cover (bottom); Corbis/Richard Hamilton Smith, 4 (foreground); Corbis/Roger Ressmeyer,
18–19; Corbis/Scott Stulberg, 12–13; Corbis/zefa/Frank Krahmer, 28 (top); Corbis/zefa/Gary Salter,
16; Digital Stock, 10; Digital Vision, 9, 21; Getty Images Inc./The Image Bank/Mike Brinson, 25; Getty
Images Inc./The Image Bank/Steve Niedorf Photography, 24; James P. Rowan, 28 (bottom); Minden
Pictures/Pete Oxford, 22–23; Peter Arnold, Inc./Klein, 11; Shutterstock/Andy Lim, 29 (top); Shutterstock/
David Woods, 29 (middle); Shutterstock/Johan Swanepoel, 27; Shutterstock/Mihhail Triboi, cover (top)

Note to Parents, Teachers, and Librarians

Where Words uses color photographs and a nonfiction format to introduce readers to the vocabulary
of space. *Near and Far* is designed to be read aloud to a pre-reader, or to be read independently by
an early reader. Images and activities encourage mathematical thinking in early readers and listeners.
The book encourages further learning by including the following sections: Table of Contents, Fun Facts,
Glossary, Read More, Internet Sites, and Index. Early readers may need assistance using these features.

Table of Contents

What Is Near? What Is Far?

Something near is close to you.
Something far is away from you.

Cows that are near are easy to see. Cows that are far are harder to spot.

People look bigger
when they are near.

6

People look like dots
when they are far.

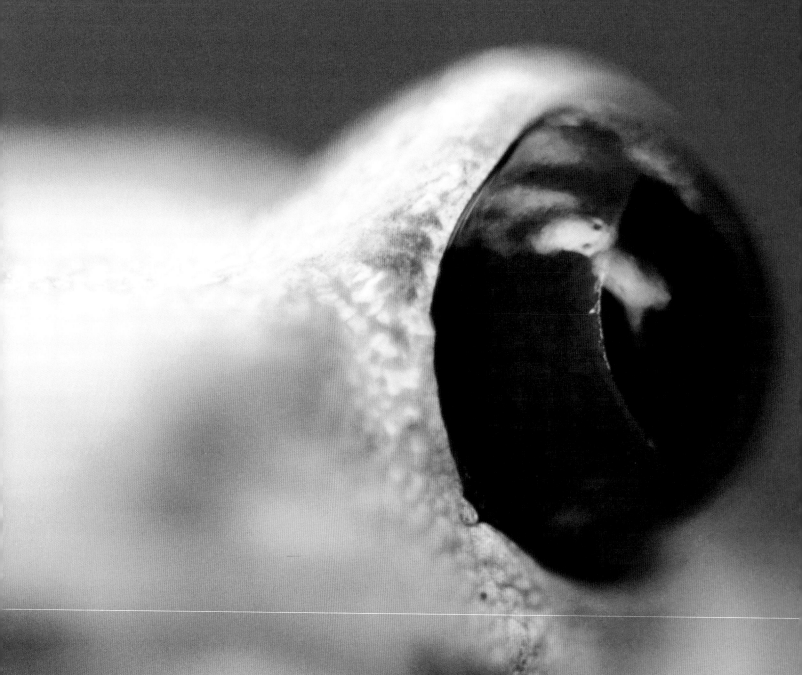

When something is very near to you, it's hard to tell what it is.

But when it is far enough away,
it's easy to see it's a frog.

When you are near an ostrich,
you can see the fuzzy feathers
on its head.

When an ostrich is far from you,
you can see its long neck and legs.

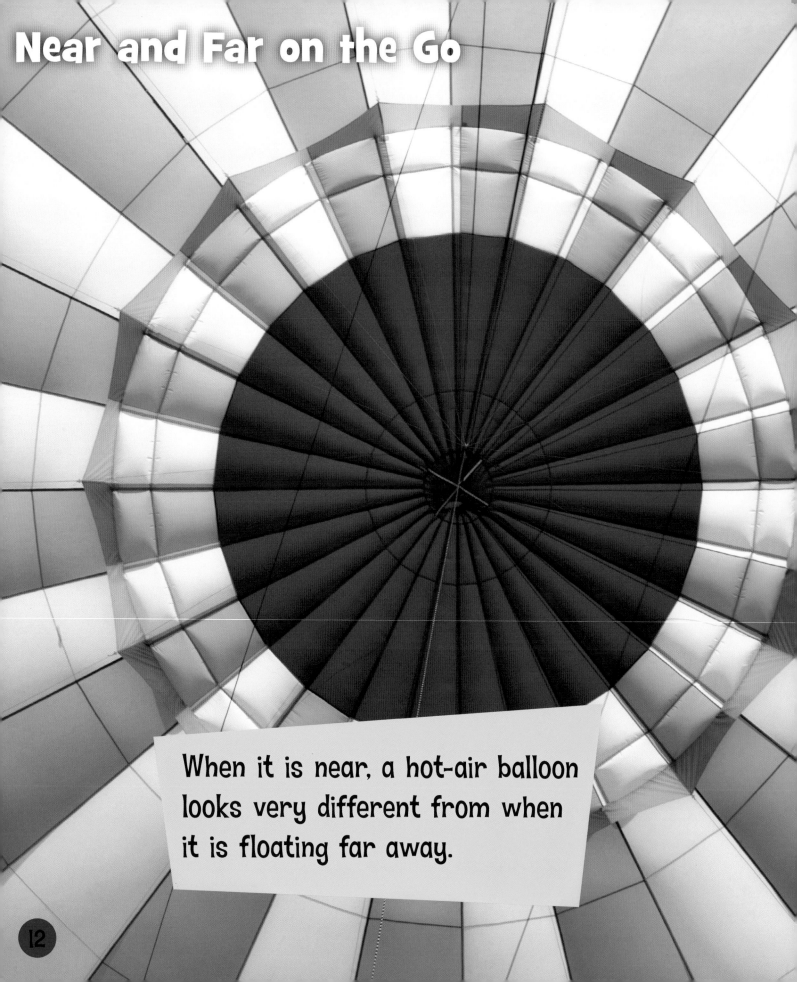

Near and Far on the Go

When it is near, a hot-air balloon looks very different from when it is floating far away.

Balloons stay near as long as you
hold tightly to their strings.

Let go of the balloons, and
they will float far away.

When you travel near your home,
a bicycle is the way to ride.

For travel far away, an airplane is the way to go.

How far can something go? Spaceships travel as far away as anyone has ever been able to go.

What Is Better, Near or Far?

Baby animals are safest near
their mothers.

Cape buffalo try to stay far away from hungry lions.

Some animals we like to have
near us.

24

Would you want to be near these
animals? No, stay far away!

Near and Far Facts

Baby kangaroos, called joeys, stay very near their mothers. After birth, a joey crawls inside its mother's pouch. When the joey is about 8 to 10 months old, it is able to leave its mother's pouch and hop about.

Baby sea turtles hatch on land and have to crawl far across the beach to reach their ocean home. Years later, many females return to the same beach to lay their own eggs.

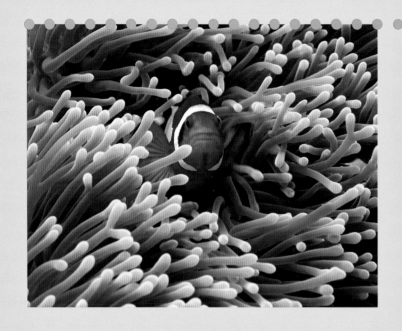

The clown fish stays near the sea anemone plant while other fish stay far away. The anemone's tentacles kill other fish that touch them. But the clown fish's body protects it from the anemone's deadly tentacles.

The moon is nearer to earth than anything in space. But it is so far away that you would have to travel all the way around the world more than 40 times to equal the distance from the moon to earth. So, what do you think? Is the moon near or far?

Something that is at arm's length is near. How many things can you reach out and touch right now? How many things are more than an arm's length away?

Glossary

airplane (AIR-plane)—a machine with an engine and wings that flies through the air

fuzzy (FUHZ-ee)—covered with short, soft hairs

hot-air balloon (HOT-air buh-LOON)—an aircraft with a very large bag filled with hot air or gas, with a basket for carrying passengers

ostrich (OSS-trich)—a large African bird that can run very fast but cannot fly

spaceship (SPAYSS-ship)—a spacecraft designed and built to travel into space

tentacle (TEN-tuh-kuhl)—a thin, flexible arm on some animals

travel (TRAV-uhl)—to go from one place to another; to take a trip.

zebra (ZEE-bruh)—a wild animal similar to a horse but smaller with black and white stripes on its body

Read More

Crews, Nina. *A High, Low, Near, Far, Loud, Quiet Story.*
New York: Greenwillow Books, 1999.

Fox, Mem, and Judy Horacek. *Where Is the Green Sheep?* Orlando: Harcourt, 2004.

Johnson, Tami. *Above and Below.* Where Words.
Mankato, Minn.: Capstone Press, 2007.

Internet Sites

FactHound offers a safe, fun way to find Internet sites related to this book. All of the sites on FactHound have been researched by our staff.

Here's how:

1. Visit *www.facthound.com*

2. Choose your grade level.

3. Type in this book ID **0736867368** for age-appropriate sites. You may also browse subjects by clicking on letters, or by clicking on pictures and words.

4. Click on the **Fetch It** button.

FactHound will fetch the best sites for you!

Index